Movement
Through
Depth

by

BRENDAN TRIPP

ON JOURNEYS NEWLY MADE

rails extend through time
the "el" carries me north
    abstraction becomes
    all the earth
    a world of views
    extracted, vague
    set in some haze
    within the mind

familiar sights are taken by
I ride alone through minor crowds
    the words
    are not sufficient
    memory does not allow
    the flowering of night
    caught in image
    in crystal set

places long ago are cut
by movement in this present light
    almost expecting
    faces lost
    to make return in this
    I lose their names
    I lose my own
    to this decay of life

the sun bleeds westward, draining day
as appointments call the northward flow
    bits fly by
    kaleidoscopic
    the tide now cycles
    ever inward
    making up a change of life
    tearing at the poisoned soul

termination heralds its approach
with visions of eternal trials
    cards are dealt
    against the dark
    allotting facts
    and places to the eye
    so like the final blade
    dividing will from flesh

THE BROKEN OF THE OLD

and what has leaning
and what bears cause
there seen so few places
that give us entrance
that allow
a shedding of these chains
and a lifting of the veil
that holds us blindly
in some self-inflicted night
not free to open
not loose enough to spin
the visions that we know
deep within the mind

somehow
a crucial piece goes missing
a gap intrudes
that all our currents
can not jump
an emptiness invades the place
that would allow
the forming of new worlds

it all drops down to words
that swirl around
the nexus of intent
never reaching
the focus of our thought
never knowing
the crystal sharpness
that spreads across the night
and so infects
all other minds with light
so powerful
so clean

perhaps a death
should have become before
a sweeping tide to bring
reforming dark
        to take the scattered bits of I
        and cast then on the winds of time
        to settle in another place
        not burdened with a broken soul
perhaps a leaving
ran on some other line
that came and went
within some daylight
within some long ago
in better places
in sweeter fate

OUR LAND UNFROSTED

these are
we are
not those
they are of the fields and forest
they know seasons and their pulse
we are
solid
we are frozen steel
we have mighty concrete muscles
that tear away the trees and grass
and make things grey
purified and still
they do not wake
they do not see
the brutal rise of dawn
splash red and orange on thrusting spires
as sky-born lamps cede to their master's day
on silent streets
on sidewalks wet from night
no, they do not know,
these other ones,
they live with life
and breathe the puling of its ways
their mornings come with waking things
that scream the beatitudes of earth
before they start the killing dance
of the feeding and the fed
we are
so far
so driven from those ways
as morning brings the surging race
in sweats of madness
headlong in an alloy dream
so tightly focused to be gone
into the realms of sun-seared night
we are
the real
not like
the simpering course of man
locked crying in the garden's ash

LOST BETWEEN DAYS

these are places
defining distance
the hollow shells
of far aways
yet these too fall
under the sway of self
and lie corrupted
below the open moon

the prayer of breaking
seems absurd
against those phantom ego chains
the shell is massive
hideous and strong
yet through its fractures
we glimpse that crystal light
and so struggle on

towards this leaving
we have gone
made voyages to nights beyond
the balance of the day
we are anticipation
a quiver and a hope
that by this shadow lighting
real change may plant a seed

it almost comes to ending
almost reaches cycles through
the gates of time
sketched into fullness by the miles
taken out to wider ways
that may yet blossom
to bear the fruit
of life repurified

TO BLINDED MOVE UNGUIDED

from there we move on
taking abrupt the bitter pill,
seed to prayer,
and in confession make new maps
and pen the world afresh

I seek the blade
to sever all this clinging life
which hangs putrescent
wrapping with decayed embrace;
there must be clearness,
these must be clean,
lopped smoothly from the growing limb

how does one speak
this banishing?
how do the words create
that separation
and forge such absence as would free
the soul from grasping shell?

it knows that well
by symbols deep within,
yet utters silence to the plea,
hooded, stark,
as though expectant of some sign
to open tomes
and light the way to probing minds

thus steel the centers
and so invoke
the lineage of all our tribe
to shed this darkness
and pierce the veil of future life

BLEED CHANNELS OF THE MIND

there stands the absence
switched over by the chronicle
of departed things coming back
drifting soundly though the distance of the night
contained in darkness
all discomforts of wrong time
confusing thought in shallow grasp
that knows nothing of the real

this comes up acid
like vomit on the walls of no control
etching maladies in the record of the place
scenting years with trails of pain
which reels in remembering
somehow vague, hazy, blurred
a sea of scenes through which to swim
to find the truth of history

stuttering events decay
each to their individualistic frame
held outside the flow of time
as though a window to the world
not linked by bricks into a whole
these float in limbo
and can not build a life
or forge a course of being

this state is poison
damaged and unwell
all growth is pruned to death
all vitalness is drained away
we are abstraction
a theory and not real
as though our dreamer
had lost the reins of sleep

still there occurs the breaking
where madness rips the steel of tawdry day
like thunder tearing clear blue skies
and shocks the open gaping eyes
of robot clowns to vision
cry for this seeing
weep oceans for this violation
of reality and stares

IN CHAPELS OF THE FLAME

too much comes
in distant time
mind is washed
away by action
special places
focus in the light
luminescence
grips the soul
shining strangely
bringing all to change

ritual moves
within these circle bounds
fire and crystal
invade the night
vistas are unveiled
to the seeking eye
that rides the lines
of deeper inner sight
awash in color
shifting beyond form

drums sound in sanctums
of dance and chant
selves are abandoned
to meld as one
running united
into arcane plans
isolation splits
into a whole
arriving fearless
awash in light

other eyes
pierce these shadows
they set the stage
on which we play
their names are hidden
their world arcane
yet on this path
does mastery lie
just beyond
the striving of our grasp

YET MISSING YOUR EMBRACE

almost there
and yet so far
into my darkness
you descend
to sit with me
and travel these few lines
of history preserved

is this a step
on new paths
forged in passion's wish,
or only dreams
gone false and hollow
empty in the ancient curse
within my life?

you are softness
yet do not yield
you move away
smiling at my reaches
retreating from my grasp
in subtle fading
distant and denied

shadows lurk,
the doubts and fears
of long rejected time
form a mist
a haze of inky dusk
that clouds my mind and heart
when turned to you

is this loving,
can there be love
in these shallows of my pain?
I am an ache
a craving based on you
confused and empty
not knowing where to turn

SMUDGED WITHIN DAY

sleeps stashes off these moments
thickness, heaviness
invade the senses
making all things vague
in and out of reason
we shift down from reality
and cross the ghostly line
to other places
other certainties
other worlds where to be confused
uncertain and at sea
to act out all the lives of dreams
shallow dreams
based on lines
floating off mid-sentence sense
or themed by distant TV voice
not quite shut out
not quite let in
to clearly follow
as form of data outside held
not wholly centered here
in new worlds
strangely set apart
abutting daytime
just slightly off its edge
to fallen sides of pages
hung suspended by a thread
to where we were
and who we are
not built on distant histories
that waking question
and seem too real
to be cast off as only dreams
as names return
in written time
perhaps by several days set off
but yet returned
from months and years removed
they come back
echoing from the call of dreams
splitting reason at the seams
pressing into daylight world
a fading placement
a phone line draining
of the seen

PALE ENDINGS FOUND IN BLACK AND GREY

darkness creeps
over absent fields
the cities
are in shadow
their buildings
shrouded in despair
deserted
void in twilight vague
winds howl
screaming half lit
unfettered cross the plane
tearing dust from sand
sand from stone
blasting structure
dimming glass
pummeling a grey
grey world
granite in light
charcoal in its shade
ebbing edges
blurring line
churning at
the dirty clouds
roiling through
disrupted skies
unwell unyielding
locking in
the secret death
the hidden plague
which lies unmoving
amid the trash
the piles of brick
and shattered steel
hid in some dark
locked down
in dimmer haze

BLURRED BY THE TACHY RIDE

sight of motion
racing within the head
hurtling past phrases
visions built of sound and light
not quite whole
cloaked in darkness like the screen
untriggered status
unset locus of the stream
flashing towards some central point
vanishing in infinities
all is speed
and motive pressings into states
made more like violence
tactilely banking through these turns
with observing eyes within
almost ripping from the skin
into some new dimension's arms
grey like pages moved too fast
bent in light twisted
funnel mirrors presentation
rattling the now spewing text
against the twitching mind
as all slides past
and numbers rotate ever up
gauges toting up the marks
of strange attainment
and measurements still undefined
dashing into future lines
in consecrations of the past
culled from rituals of need
the ebbing currents of the word
within the backwash of our life
that billows in its myriad forms
of cloud and foam and smoke and steam
and then shoot by
tearing somehow at the head
spinning consciousness to set
in focus on the tunnel seen
with accelerating drive
streaming, blurring
into indistinction
uncatchable, untamed

WRONG ENTRY, WRONG INSIDE

dawn abruptly cuts the night
and enters to the palace
dark hallways beckon with their age
towards secrets in the murk
this is the seat of the abyss
its massive pull rings from the walls
       its presence everywhere
       within the keep is felt

scratches have abused the sheen
of marble and the polished stone
smooth surface marred with warning signs
the dying words of those before
etched for the ages
mute screams against our step
       here never to be heard
       and never to be seen

somewhere behind the ears
now floats a tune's vague line
familiar, calling to the mind
beyond location
somehow set off as in the soul
not placed or truly grasped
       whose action plays this reed
       that ushers us inside?

the patterns on the floor
erupt to number too correct
and stun perception's sight
all aspects fall into their place
as though again a trap had sprung
within the master plan
       new darkness folds across
       a morn too briefly light

IN MASS DERIVED OF HEAT

dry comes the heat
and echoes of the future place
folded in return
days now past and days to come
we greet them
spreading knowledge
offering the mode to be
sending into vectored night
the distant spans' locale
this is the seeding
the open oven door
set in skies to desiccate
the dusty land
pouring sweat from fainting brows
on the trail of common ease
now straining at the task
wondering what comes
in long day walkings
new journeys we will make
in the sere and powdered ground
baked solid in the sun
as so we sleep
or try to sleep
and live until the dark
streaming precious water lost
to ever thirsty air
hiding for the ritual
unspoken and unsure
anticipating what might be
under the canopy of stars
cut by winds uncaring
not knowing what these are
or of ourselves
what names we have
pronounceable by night
there is a sullen thickness here
a mass built of the heat
which grips the avenues
of midday concrete motion
and makes all going slow
defying the equating mind
to define its lines of grasp
the bends and folds
now grow complex
as time shuttles in between
the simmer and the fade

THE BLOOD OF DARKNESS, THE BILE OF LIGHT

dig down deep
through the hours
and excavate
the ashes of the day:
    here lie the secrets
    and the patterns
    lost to life,
    broken pieces
    of intention,
    and fragments
    of these shattered hopes
    strewn in layers
    defying plan

(hollow chambers
wait below,
the void of anguish
denied all time)

futility
builds up its marks
describing platforms
of the pyre
    there are reasons
    somewhere within,
    purpose hiding
    beyond some distant wall
the tribe is marching
to this place,
the sacrifice
can now be made
    and lo, the die is cast,
    the victim chosen
    as in a nightmare
    always self

(this knowing
does the one no good;
no paths are open,
no actions are sustained)

    Here comes seeing
    borne on night
    here arrives
    the virtue hearing
    all within the dark...

FEELING THROUGH THE VEILS OF SELF

what runs through
the mind
scraps of stuff
picked up here and there
tunes and words
pulled from stories
newspapers, magazines
and these books
we always read
forming images and swirls
in kaleidoscopic sound
    this is the upper level
    the flow of data
    like a text

also there runs through
the self
a different line
this is flavored
with emotion's taint
and speaks of panic
anxiety and fear
it is built
of strangled hopes,
love shattered on the rocks
of crumbled aspirations
    this is the middle level
    the flow of anguish
    like lost blood

sometimes this runs through
the gut
a pulse, a charge,
a gripping press of speed
which kicks to mania
and opens up
those other states
which have been too long estranged
cloaked by acid tinged with dread
blocked from being
in the world
    this is the central level
    the flow of passion
    like hot wires

ANCIENT REASON AT THE LAST

times derive of shaking crystal
shudder, shatter
enveloping the course to take

      encircle now
      the tail and beak
      make whole the round
      and so return

we can not take the offered road
distant, dismal
into these discarded passings

      hold up to sky
      the blade of night
      transmute to grace
      the deity

the moment's pressing comes unstemmed
rushing, reeling
to force the hand dividing life

      swing censers round
      the altar's reach
      to focus will
      into the act

within regret solidifies
blocking, blasting
formed of scars on broken hearts

      crash into void
      the mind drops down
      emotion drowns
      in seas of dread

denied a recourse to clean ways
blissful, blessing
the broken soul reverts to pasts

      march to gallows
      strewn with flowers
      tis the season
      when all must die

UNWHOLESOME WORLD, SO WORSE THAN DEATH

somewhere inside
curled up
shaking through the spasms
of systems riding through
the agony of life...

      nothing is right
      the universe bleeds
      springs of decay

expenditures all outflow
from dollars to emotion
they fade to void
and build a gap within
there is no return
no inward flowing feed
this soul is dying
trapped in a vampire world
which saps the vital spark
and plunges my perceptions
into blackness
draped with death

      nothing is good
      and everything seeks
      to murder joy

the trap is sprung
and reality gives us no escape
all things have edges
sharp, cutting,
dimensions turn acute
to bring us pain
moisture beads on brows
and turns to acid
stripping off still sensate flesh
in sheets of seething gore
the air itself
thickens, gels
holds us in some amber gas
which poisons us for some display
in sadist sideshows
the form and being of this place
      this grinding center
      this unholy cavern
      this damned unceasing cage

POINTS TO PLACEMENT FORMING

1
we are asked of these distances
and are dumbfounded
blank with naught to say
2
rage smears from darkness and neglect
swords flash mighty
as they stab and stab again
3
before the dissolution comes
there is a reminiscence
of new place and pointlessness
4
we stand here empty
as with a broken toy
and know not how the all was lost
5
all good things become the victim
of the sorrow and despite
that warp the universe's turns
6
at times belief is not withheld
and traps form from the air
but not again, no not again
7
the tones of flesh and curves of form
blast echoes through the mind
yet falling through the years they fade
8
have stars spoken on the page
and charted out the form of night
into these unknown lands?
9
time bleeds sickly into dust
and hands us things of stone
all but to go, all but to go
10
there is denouncement's path
sharp and hard to take while sane
yet boiling to the blood
11
because of thee they all lack voice
and nameless they become
for these are halls of thine alone
12
and so is done the seeding
as dictates are obeyed
reality bows down to will

SWEPT UP WITHIN THAT RUSHING TIDE

"I would find the places
where they sleep more lightly,
as I sleep more lightly;
I would awake, oh, God, I would awake! "

these spirits
come again,
their visitations
hit hard within my life;
they are as
an unknown star
whose tidal pull
tears all my will away
in the violence of its wake
            and I am bled out,
            naked to the other side,
            angry and unsure,
            unable to see,
            unable to know,
            blinded and beset by winds,
            adrift on turgid seas

                    if such is brought
                    by preparation,
                    how much more
                    shall enter in the act?

there is a flow
in this ride,
I feel a pattern
leading on
            as days fall into the abyss,
            emptying on cataracts of time
there shall be journals kept there,
I feel explosions of the word
now pending to be born,
awaiting in the wings
for hours of discomfort,
for cold distressing time
            the tribe is pulled around,
            the lineage retained
in this might come
the focus of release
in the season of return
at locations of desire,
in this might come
the strengthening
against that day-lit night

OUT THROUGH THOSE REALMS OF SIGHT

for this is the manner
in which the past is retrieved
    pulled from nightmares
    simmering in the juices
    of a psyche gone awry
lines erupt
and go faulty
eyes stare wildly
at distances not attained
thoughts careen
from infinity to the grave
and hold a vigil
sweaty in the palm of time
    this is the entrance
    the vale of knives
    through these doorways
    have passed all those who see
no ground supports me
no haven shields my mind
I am all pulse
an organism wildly paced
run ragged, naked, and insane,
beholden only to that drive
insistent, forward, on and on
    steel congeals to challenge stone
    all is cutting, acid, sharp,
    the form inverts, in to out,
    cadaver gruesome yet alive
here there is folding
here dimensions cease and bend
senses shift to other nodes
and every vector realigns
    cardinals, where are you now,
    familiar spirits lose their shape
    directions shatter in vortex drag
over here
over there
sense still mingles
amid the chaos, madness, whirl
there is a center
somehow a self
within this forms a point of mind
which reaches out to grasp the world
and in its reach
encompasses the whole
    no lines now
    no demarcations
    there is no other apart from self
    no holding, held,
    no seer, seen

against the churning
memory attains
scatter-shot reason
whole histories detailed
spun into lineages beyond time
repeated, redoubled,
branched in layers in nameless states
which curl and curl
back on themselves
becoming altered, becoming changed
yet standing into unique space
unlabeled, undefined
     each universe is born herein
     no meaning bides in time
     eternal, momentary
     clicking through durationless
and this, and here
the mists relieve
again the form clears out
to old, familiar,
and mundane worlds
not shifted in their lines
     so, too, the problem,
     perhaps the curse
     that from the outer bounds returns
     to one again
     always the first

TO HURT, TO DIE, TO KILL

1
so, there it is
and there it goes
as hell's incited
all the night
to visions of the scream
made inward,
hollow,
empty in the soulless void
killed off by days
of grind and chain
and by rejection,
spite of the demeaning race,
heard again in silent words
unspoken yet still felt
by tattered heart
so gird by scars
that it amazes by the pain
as though by now it could not feel
could not fall twisted
by these blades
of offhand killing hate
spit out in nights of foolish hope
in waking dreams of good
as though the curse would lift
and bliss enter this life

stupid fool, idiot,
accursed you are, accursed remain,
and accursed you still shall be;
for nothing lifts the veils of death
which darken all your dreams,
nothing spares your dying soul
from the tortures of false day,
and nothing clears the damning lien
of anguish on your heart

this is Hell
and you are it
damned, despised,
cast down, debased,
reviled and ridiculed,
hated and harassed,
scorned by all the caring kind,
denied the basic things of man,
in ashes dragged
yet forced to live
to breathe and toil
within the shadows of the walls
of the exiled Eden
forever taunting
forever giving pain

2
you stare in nights unrested
stare at ceilings,
stare at walls,
all press in screaming
and allow no sleep
all drive home barbs
of how you fail and fail
of how your loneliness,
your solitude, continues
unabated through the years
on cycles run of blind false hope
and the crashing mass of absence
dropped crushing with the total weight
of reality's sudden sight

damned, you are damned,
you stare in sleepless anguish
and know that you are damned,
you pray for death,
you touch the blade
and pray for will to come to hands
to rip the flesh,
to tear the veins,
to rend the life-force from your form
and make you free
a soul cut loose
from all these killing ties to life
which seek to snuff the surer spark
which suffocates within

as those hours
drain towards day
your thoughts become a dirge
bewailing changes made to life
once in destruction's way;
were I to know
how all these years
would unfold from the past
never would I ever stop
the use of drugs and drink,
yes, had I known
the way these years
would hack apart my soul,
I would so redouble
all abuse
and die before these days
had chance to dawn
in sickening colors to these eyes
so full of anguish,
so wracked with pain,
so broken and dismayed,
much better to have died back then
than to ever see
these killing days
in which my soul now bleeds

3

know this dying is desired
and let the world be murdered
see the killing in their eyes
and from their ways be sundered

purge the self of common ways
and enchain yourself to sight
cast off caring for the day
and be suckled by the night

take to form of supermen
both the fabled and foretold
slay all weakness held within
let your blood run icy cold

forge a virtue out of hate
make a weapon out of rage
let the chaos bring you joy
in the destruction of the age

tear out the caring softness
make your soul a thing of steel
take power as your life force
and make strength the thing you feel

yes, turn their curse against them
for their hatred bring them Hell
when that breaking comes within
you must surely use it well

if love's to be denied me
if from pleasure I'm exiled
how long will ego suffer
before vengeance will run wild?

OF STORMS AMONGST THE STORM

1
there is darkness
spread over the earth
old gods are rising
to manifest their rage
in thunder, blackness,
wind and stars they come
and shake the puny towers
of the modern world
2
a darkness too
hangs on my soul
a blackness sinks roots
deep within my heart
      a place of death this is
      a place of killing what's inside
there are no tomorrows
seen good within this cage
         3
        hatred enters
        in this place,
        rage has blinded
        the caring eye;
        no rules have I,
        no laws, no mores,
        all comes to massing
        for an end
4
all should drown
in storms like these
a washing should make clean
      crash shudders the street
      echoes on walls
      reverberates in shadowed spirit
we cast against the winter's will
and duck again its freeze
in moments clutching safety
5
break again the bonds of mind,
tear off logic's sticky mantle
and cast them from the parapets
into the roiling mass below;
there may be freeing in this chain
there may yet come release
born out of madness and despite
which lashes at its makers

OF WHAT NOT ME IS ME

there shadows another life,
black and white pictures
and magazine ads
bring this close,
almost surfacing in the mind;
somewhere behind
the conscious flow
this is lived
     is experienced
     is known
somewhere beneath
the dire banalities of these days
that other course is made

what other name
is held there,
what other face is borne
to strip that world into its subjects
and strand in different distance
the eyes' unknowing stare?
     a gravity pulls
     at me from there
     I seek the way to turn
          to see

sometimes I fear the looming
of some future leaning back through time
to speak to me, to warn
     movie scenes detail this
     in visions that are not my own
and I am lost
in insufficient data
all at sea
in the twisting lines
of descending possibilities
unsure and guessless
confused by haunting skies

A BALANCE FRAGILE KEPT

I see this abyss
I see these cliffs
I see the void on which to step
to live by flying
and not by fear
    below there is flame
    and churning seas of molten stone
conflagrations of fury beckon
vertigos that seek revenge
against those few who dare exist
aspiring heights beyond old reach
    there must be trusting,
    the pathway is unmarked
    and by most eyes unseen
upon the road of emptiness
the foot hesitates, unsure,
the lower form so dreads the fire
it fights the higher will
        something within needs to press on
        into the swirling insubstantial black

and so it dawns
this point of life
a balance held
between a soaring
and a plummet down
    this is the interval unshocked
    awaiting aid from finer realms

        there is no guiding
        but to go
        there are no reasons
        that will stand
        there is no teaching
        that will lead
        there are no options
        but to act

perhaps the time
enfolds the guise
of mastery beyond the veil
which reaches out
from in our dark
to steer our fledgling steps

THE PICTURES AND THE WING

it locks up
and locks down
without motion
divided from a sense of going
                these are not angels
                here allowed
forgetting washes many waves
and in many ways makes clean
the slate of mind
      not good, this clean,
      not purified
these are the rivers of the drowned
the dried stream beds awaiting rain
that never answers in the night
cold desert night that freezes dry
           I am in this scene
           I shiver restless
           and fear the darkness lurking
                there are no footsteps
                but there are footsteps
                there is no breathing
                but there is breath
and still I lose the names
the years of study are all for naught
when nothing opens to the mind
in shifting searches of panic's want
      who knows the order
      that make hierarchies sing?
this too drops down
the easy words fall with the rest
communication then erodes
to shallows stagnant in the ebb
left with no essence, jewels, or shine
           are there no growings,
           no forms of change
           that might allow release?
the long, long night
still marches on,
the troops still press against the dark
(brave boys, yet stupid, and somehow sad)
and ring with sorrow
the very form which makes the fight
                it drops here then
                while being this,
                formed in reversion
                and accidental light

THINGS FORESHADOWED, BROKEN WITHIN

1
dwindling through the final hours
given fill of scenes and sights
this sets
it settles
like ashes dropping through the sea
or states of being splitting off
as water into ice
or water into steam
2
time comes for changing
or to return
but worlds move on in other cycles
that will not mesh with single wheels
and must spin difference,
motion, growth,
or new decay torn at old living
brought into violent ways
3
strange agendas pull at threads
in silent chambers of the mind,
this music threatens all our sleep
to follow dreams
and streams of lies
into the swirling web of night
set with enticements, sound and shine
against the pattern of our life
4
I see square one,
loops batter time back to this place,
I see the forming of the disk,
the broken turning of existence
which never grows,
which knows no progress,
just shattered promises denied
in this sickening return
5
because of habit there is darkness,
because of living there is death,
out of ignorance
a storm cloud brews
foreshadowing a sense of doom;
where can enlightenment give shelter
to tide till age of light
breaks in a new found dawn?

PART AWAY, PART ABSENT

1
comported with discretion
what has been distant
falls down the years
and into here and into now
2
kaleidoscopes are within
the screen-form of my eyes,
impressions feed the soul
strange meats of color set
3
anger sputters, seeking ignition,
too long have struggles countered
in the soiling of the whiteness,
too much has rage to run on pyres upon this night
4
we divide the ancient histories
into pathways we might tread,
we spin these knives against our time
and wait for bits and slices to scatter on the floor
5
name the places of the blood
and privilege denied;
across these lines there lies a land
of gleaming power felt
6
familiar in the unknown,
we must chase after the strange
aching for some foreignness
too weird to be met sane
7
badness lurks within us;
a worm of discontent
eats tunnels through the soul,
drips poison on the heart
8
the questions of who inside, who out
go misty, blurred, confuse like fog
swept chilling across the fields of self
and blind us to the outlines of the sun

CARVED FROM UNYIELDING STATES

these mirrors are useless,
they can not show
that wisdom depth behind the eyes,
we wait for calls
from eyes that see
to summon to some other land
and service to the spirit's light

all is fractured
in our world,
bits and flakes are littered here
and no whole is
for us to see,
to grasp as one
in unity

good and bad now overlap
on sliding scales of moral tides,
there is no leading
for the heart
amid this grey and foggy zone
which has no standard
or rock on which to cling

these thoughts go screaming
through the inky void
like signals searching
for receivers tuned
into their wavelength,
into perceptions
equal to their world

names flip in and out of mind,
hope drives nails into the heart
that this solitude
might not be whole,
and that the exile
might have banishment removed
and know the company of his kind

AWAITING DAYS

when those days come
they shall come with change
with alteration
and new manners for to be

when those days come
they will arrive with fire
a cleansing fire
that shall not burn
except to tear away the stain
that marks this life
as one delayed

when those days come
they will be soaked in light
a piercing light without a name
which floods from centers
of the soul
and opens up the eyes to see
what has been arcane

when those days come
they come on winds
which blow from mountains in the north
that sweep the deserts in their heat
that move across the face of seas
and stir the jungles of the night
to scour new ways
from out the old

when those days come
they come to be

THE DREAM STATES OF THE DAY

we drag ourselves through deserts
our fingers bleed from scrabbling
over grit and dirt and rocks
the sun beats down without forgiveness
denying respite in our pleas
and seeks our searing death
                              again we wake
                              and wonder when

on mountainsides we freeze
our muscles ache against the strain
of upward climbing
to palaces just glimpsed in mists
the holy halls of answers deigned
to end our searching quests
    but talons reach
    and sharp beaks tear
    and there is falling
    plummeting to depths
                              again we stir
                              and question where

we find ourselves adrift
deep amid a green expanse
which swallows all
we seek to probe the murk with eyes
which are now useless holes in bone
stripped in sinking through the darkness
                              again we surface
                              and ponder how

above the clouds we take to flight
held precipitous within movement
given vistas in strange sequence
beyond horizon's ken
        forms are made as by a net
        strung of jewels on jewels within
        a matrix of oome ulliei gems
        we seek to touch
        but in our reaching all dissolves
        and melts away to void
                              again we rise
                              enquiring why

THINGS OVERHEARD BY EARS WITHIN

1
patterns of disarray
enfold the hardened life,
new datum enters in the flow
and makes of reason
a folly fractured into time

2
I would that light take up
that brutal light,
that hideous light,
that shredding light
which strips away
all pretense, comfort, and deceit,
this beacon would I shine
against the sightless
and savor screams
as illusions melt away

3
there comes return
for those adrift,
new places come to old
and freeze fresh patterns
within the crystal's web

4
within grey stone
within old temples gone to dust
one has arrived
a silent one who now prepares
the voices of the age
his rites are simple, ancient, sharp,
and hone the course of future days
awaiting echoes of command
within the silence
the cold and awesome dawn

5
so, there you know the seeing,
the seeing long denied,
a wave now gathers far away
amassing power, accruing mass
that soon shall sweep these ledgers clean

FLOWED FROM SOME PATCHWORK QUILL

from the harbors of division
into the cataclysm's rise
there are churnings in the temper
and the temporal flow of life

> yet we wait
> pondering the absence of the gods
> biding time
> for some desired return
> both mythic and innate

this
is out,
not allowed,
empty and void,
frantic and insane,
run to missing,
held vacant.
hollow,
gone

> heaven answers
> not at all
> doesn't seem to
> hear our call
> grace got scuttled
> in the fall
> love has dwindled
> very small

a spear of panic splits the soul
and skewers thought against its grind
tearing back the skin of reason
and bleeding off the broth of will

> pardon,
> please pardon;
> there seems nothing left,
> nothing held against this time,
> so little for this crop of days
> which fall unwanted into pasts
> forgotten before passing...
> pardon this
> and pardon these
> still all unknowing,
> still blind unto their crimes

PONDERED ASPECTS OF THE PAGE

pause to be with this
          words only
          words
worlds on lying wards
false confinement in the sun
                    with heat
                    beyond all sweat
sweetly singing concepts sung
                    barbs that stung
                    within, among
there are shiftings
here abouts
there are movements
mainly out
          cloaked in pretense
          veiled in lies
          they will find out
          by and by
containment is the content
is the holder of the held
                              pronounce it
                              as you may
                              it becomes
                              the street brought out of dreams
we set out the order of the order
fill the lines
and check the box
                into it is
                intuitive
                who dares to state the state
predict attenuation
the tuner tune
direction from response regret
and space the cause of change
                              this is primal
                              it changes over time
                              lives between two worlds
within divisions of the race unaltered
received unbidden in the day
comes this to me, and so it speaks
of sets directed at the way
          this looks so hard
          a brutal hand upon the stone
          that we unknowing go into
          without assenting
          forgoing sleep

PARTICLES OF THE DELAY

untoward incision
into this stream
   abject objection
   injected herein
these fritter and decay
fall into dust and blow away
      we've seen this movie
      we know this jive
still false prayers aspire
still hope
wraps cloaking papers on the loss
   disguising the lack
   from first decree
   but outlines soon surface
   of tell-tale lumps on scan
and you know of those lies
and you know of the luring
but the hook looks tasty
and the bait so sweet
   gild these arms
   gild these hands
   we are the golden, led off to be fleeced
ego, ego, one-two-three,
there are fine levels
within this deceit
     like,
     how do you separate
     the falsehood without
     from the falsehood within?
such is abrading
between these worlds
such the friction
gone to heat
   fire allows this nastiness
   fire of days ahead
but, wait, don't speak of time,
old Chronos goes unmentioned
in the valley of the sun
     on screen for
     now unseen
however there are not enough
of self to go around
   coagulate as one
   collaborate the ending
netherworlds are fine
to absent and believe

DISENCUMBERED OF THE DREAM

fortress of delusion,
held up in killing light
    there is no shelter in these walls
    no way to skip this burning

            roads present violence,
            tapes play from bones
                recalling impact
                reliving pain
            there is no context given,
            no placement and no time

we turn the symbols over,
shift and order as decreed
    your name is in this cycle
    and its pattern speaks your face

                    calls shatter,
                    unneeded breakage
                    crumbles the distance;
                    acid spews out
                    to poison the day

actions are not specific,
items are not precise
        all these harbor depths
        beyond the reach of eyes
mind flips between levels
and reels amid the spin

        pardon is pleaded,
        excuse is sought
                but there is nowhere left to hide
                all universes are patrolled

spikes impale the face through eyes
beseeching change of venue
                new colors pour through vision
                no longer bringing care
forms explode and atomize
only to reform unaltered

                    awaking,
                    now awake to day
                    not run to dying:
                    there are reprieves
                    gifted in new light

THE OLDEST SEARCH AT HAND

I search for you
but find you not,
    I am broken inside
    and can not open wide enough
    to take within the scope of earth,
    to spread these arms in an embrace
    that swallows up the universe

Where are you?
Why do you hide?

I chain myself to second days
in hopes to find a clue of you,
    I am amazed
    at the volume of the lore I see,
    the empty husks you have cast off
    and left behind to suit the blind
    who care not for your sight

Where is it
that you reside?

I sometimes catch a glimpse of you
in light run tinted through thick leaves,
in patterns cast by setting suns,
and nighttime in deserted streets,
    but at perception you are gone,
    hid back behind the sorting mind
    which cuts apart the world
    and finds no whole among the bits

Are you cloaked
within plain sight?

I sometimes think you lurk inside,
somewhere beneath the veils of me,
    but blockages derail my search,
    amid that chaos, rage and pain

Where are you?
why hide from me?

I would envelop in your vastness
and bleed away the walls of self
to know your union, to be your one,
and rise within that soul again

THE BROKEN SHELLS FORGOTTEN

birds in flight
bleeding colors
monochrome city
superimposed

    days of deigning
    days of designation
    distribution is deterred
    in favor of the mode of flight

the channels are a-changin'
a hatched-up scramble through the dial
within receivers of the mind
the symbols, cymbals, and symbiotic raps

        portions are partitioned
        staged for storage
        emptied for the entry set
        for further feeding, finer fill

we teeter sickly on the edge
of being thrust to other roles
not made to purge it
not at gun-point vertigo

    lost in frustration, confusion
    the names all swirl, all swim
    they are not indexed
    within the dawn not seen

        and of unseeing, so there is
        a manner found unwilling
        we see the loss, we sound retreat
        while ruing fresh our fate

metal abides the sky
steel derives the earth
we are petrol in the flame
a motion set upon the curse

    come on then now
    throw off the husk
    peel through the station
    which marks the phases' change

THE GENESIS OF HORRID SIGHT

it is the feeling of angst
that is the voice,
it is the detached discomfort
which sparks the inner scream
    not with
    a reason,
    not with
    a name
rite is removed,
temples lie in dust;
the sacrifice is within,
gory with forbidden acts
        hideously tearing
        at the fabric of the soul
we are blinded,
lying in the pools of our own exuberance,
our own inertia,
aimed in madness and coached by lies
                they are all lies,
                all fantasies,
                these things that we believe;
                we act the fool, unhearing
                of the mocking laughter
                from the beyond
no one suspects the depths of that rage
nobody plumbs the abyss of its logic
        for life is evil
        and must be turned
        to good
and we sharpen up the knives of offering
to accost this ignorance
to refute that search for "nice"
        for in our terror there is knowledge
        and in our madness there is truth
but then darkness,
but then sleep,
as all must sleep who are that blind
and all to darkness fall
who care not for the crystal light
           burning,
           ripping at the mind
there is no safety in this world,
we breathe without a net;
        awake to knowing,
        awake to rage
bring now this vision to them all
to break apart their being
and consume their putrid night

FINDING OUT THE SITE

for this is
the tight corner of time
where the walls swoop in
and focus at a point

for this is
the dark behind the mirror
where shadows may shift
and realign the real

for this is
the habit of the damned
made to be normal
dictated by the realm

for this is
the underside of stone
seen in the rotting
known only by the late

for this is
the line of plans expressed
beyond the concept
into form and being

for this is
the matrix of our fate
sucked into whirlpools
submerged amid the depths

for this is
the mist before the dawn
that cloaks the shining
and swallows up the stars

for this is
the street without an end
where busses travel
but never stop for death

for this is
the place of our design
not pure or given
but torn from out the earth

for this is
the moment of the scream
heard in the fibers
and shredded from the need

OLD WAYS MOVING TO RETURNED NEW

down the years
recall skips
   enters abscesses
   where night has gone too clear,
   turns the corner
   of forgetting and belief
and comes to rest
on places still the same
      how much can be retrieved
      from the shambles of our age?
      this decade builds of years that flew
      beyond credulity
         and nothing fits
         and nothing moves
         and nothing seems
         the way it was
still, homing on some antique spark
we make return,
decked anew in echoes of the past
we sketch a ritual
enacting what is gone
      one form of darkness
      one form of night
      one form of simmering rage and fire
      that burst out in the drugs and sweat
      left caked upon the stone
         from this we turned
         and new roads made,
         roads to nowheres,
         slower deaths,
         less fiery and less brief
a knowledge lingers deep within
from violent age
      we know the pattern
      we trace the paths of lightning arcs
      and split the seams of quiet
      with screams within our souls
and sated with this lore
we take again the reins
of loosed abandon,
concept turned to concrete forms,
and shatter lethargy's decline
      for one returning
      for one more night
      for one explosion
      seen tearing through the dance

BLIND, UNKNOWING, HOLLOW, VOID

this blindness is interminable,
this numbness is unending;
    the dark unknowing
    runs through my marrow,
    the dull extending
    pulls at time

              once I knew
                  things,
                  subjects;
              now I am empty,
              my mind a blank

              once I was
                  sure,
                  certain;
              now I am hollow,
              without a guide

all data flows away,
all information is devalued
by being incomplete
    I am unable to attain those states
    which call to me across that gap,
    as doubt of knowing freezes will
    and crumbles my resolve
              I am paralyzed,
              I am ignorance in stone,
              I have lost the filter
              which makes up lies
              convincing that we see

        how strange a vision
        that only knows the void
        and how strange a knowing
        that only senses unknowing's span

so many seem to hold some truth
but are knit to fables, lies, and schemes
which build on themselves, accruing age
which is taken for reality:
        these falsehoods most believe

              and I am worse than that,
              as I can not believe
                  but only ask,
                  only question,
                  only ache...
              how better in their blindness
              not knowing they are blind!

I would to know
but always fail,
        fail at the first,
        fail at the last,
I am emotion-swept
and without a ground,
I study tomes without recall
and scan through wisdom without effect

                        there are some pieces missing here,
                        some faculties denied my grasp;
                        the wish can not turn on the flow
                        of knowledge from those arcane taps

        the darkness spreads
        from in my soul,
        from knowing things it can not say

        the shadow moves on to my mind
        to tinge with spite and morbid taints
        all things that pass its gates

        the will is poisoned by the shade
        dripping from existing's barbs
        and seeks in curling ever small
        to disperse the hellishness of life

blindness,
darkness,
numbness,
void,
these seem to be the elements,
the water, earth, and fire
        which build the world
        which scar the eye
        which empty out the meaning
        of all that we might be

FINAL ENTRIES, TOMES OF DREAMS

and of everything
these five remain:

      a)   Rightness.
                  all misgivings
                  come to be,
                  all our worries
                  are based on fact

      b)   Foreknowing.
                  arising, clear sight
                  appears from depths;
                  almost all knowledge
                  is in our grasp

      c)   Distraction.
                  scattered rays of light, of heat,
                  disenable,
                  entangle focus,
                  make empty, nearly vile

      d)   Anguish.
                  nights tear down
                  with hope destroyed;
                  never is allowed desire,
                  never is a prayer replied

      e)   Vision.
                  these are eyes that never shutter
                  out that killing light;
                  staring, screaming,
                  they attain the mythic stance

all other things
have gone to dust,
blown away on ageless stone:

               cruelly echo in the temple
               steps from other ages passed
               into that darkness, into the haze,
               becoming versions of the game
                       not now collapsing,
                       not ever set to age

so comes the nothingness within
and dies these patterns of the sun

THE MISTRESS OF THE PLACE BEYOND

somewhere behind are the patterns
we see or feel them swirl
sensing their motions
outlining their grids
with tactile inreachings we cannot define

there is a rhythm in that darkness
a line that pumps to form
taking volition to arms and to voice
making a future stand glassy and hard
arising awesome from the mists

ears hear musics that are not played
mind echoes beat and bass and strange drums
revolving in a space unseen
returning to a time unclocked
calling forth the warrior will

there is a feeling spilt from our insides
when the veiled seductress speaks
there is a mass that forms close by
and pulls us towards its crushing core
ejecting changed in modes of blooms

ride the tow-hook of that sway
grasp the fin and feel the dive
strap upon careening carts
that ride the byways of the sky
and tear away from common worlds

I have fallen through that sea
but knew not awaking
and knew not the dream
yet I echo distant calls
which are not the stuff of me

now scan the dials
and the gauges of control
from far below the power thunders
it wells from deep within the gut
awaiting for its flame

this place takes darkness as its side
it is a gauze stripped from light
to be a fantasy of chain
we are not of here or of this
for we hear her language far too well

SHATTERED DARKNESS NOT MADE LIGHT

when these aspects emerge
and blast against the speaking,
the record of obscuration...

when these faces unmask
and iterate against the mirror
forming pools of doubled image...

when these echoes unravel
and string to lines of soft vibration
transparently amid the void...

> so comes the dawning
> of black suns in the dark,
> a new gravitation
> built of the swell of seas

there are awaitings
beyond the portals set unknown,
there are preparings
to pattern with the force of night,
there are returnings
and modes made violent, cracked through time
> ungoverned in the wild retreat,
> flavored with all pain and hate,
> run whirlpool into arcane webs
> not taken simple to the screen
> but wide dimensions. lordly grasp,
> ancient vistas made insane
> found beaten in unsubtle grey

FROM THE BLEEDING AND THE PAIN

never the minding
never the sane
never the winding
never the same
    this becomes the absence
    this evolves the void
so annoyed
run into little distance
deep within the self
    saying:
        none of this is real
        none of this exists
        none of this matters
        none of this impinges ME
for I am hidden
well within the zone
    of untouchable isolation
    and unforgivable disdain
            but wave after wave
            crash down on the head
            there is little to save
            among all these dead
but still placement is a problem,
sites and sights fly by the mind
a travelogue of splintered slides
mixed from million billion miles
unlogged, uncharted, unordered, wild
        not seeming well
        not keeping mild
        as though some other concept kept
within the settling of the day
now made with madness
sadness and decay
        this is not
        what the wanted are
        this is not
        defined, aligned
        malicious or maligned
but that does not control the absence
that does not destroy the loss
that does not redeem the injured
or form new tissues free of scars
            within this heart
            within this soul
            within the darkness
            of this so battered mind
cast drifting on the empty sea
fallen hollow on the slag heap of the rest
    made of vision
    and shattered bits of time

APART FROM BEING. SEEN TOO FAR

strain into the reversal
of locations behind space
   there are mythic threads
   which run through here,
   fibers of description
   which weave between
   the moments of our thought
   and the moments of the real
strain at these and seek to bend
our vision into sight

      somewhere back there
      there is a different place,
      like some backstage
      where ropes and curtains hang
      and passages
      run past unfinished walls
      and wires and lights
      criss-cross the shadowed zone
      preparing the illusions
      created for the stage

perception grips so hard
on the nearly absent seam,
there must be ways to pry
and lever wide that gap
      for we are sleeping here
      lulled by subtle plays
      and brutal truth resides behind
      this gauzy edge of space
there lies our destiny,
behind the facade of this world
somehow beneath the fill of color
beyond the patterns of our touch

      some say the way
      resides within
      amid the chaos of our signals
      amongst the chatter of our minds
      the path runs strangely
      like stairways leading ever down
      opening on fields of truth
      to release us into daylight
      an Escher-shift of depth for height
      the center for the rim

IN MORBID GRAVITIES

something settles
down and down
there is a sinking
within some depth
there is dropping
from states to lower forms
something plummets
in slo-mo
dragging into tragic realms

      each direction poisons
      each quarter turn
      each eighth
      brings round new vistas
      new jagged sights
            we sit on turnings
            and pray for ease in change
            but these are acid
            and burn unspoken spite

a fold has taken
within this fabric tucked
it stresses line
and warps the pull of space
      within that darkness
      a beckoning
      amid that void a call
there is no redress
no manner of respite

      somewhere off
      beside the mind
      are other movies played
      somewhere far
      from common paths
      are mythic actions made
      somewhere near
      yet so removed
      our lives have been mislaid

there is no bottom
to this sea
no halt to our decline
each veil is broken
swirled away
one with the murky deep
      our hopes are shattered
      our prayers are lost
      our course leads to decay

THE PATTERN OF FOUL WORLDS

fortune doesn't smile
on me
fortune never smiles
        we see dreams turn bitter
        drip like acid from candy planes
        warp to nightmares of regret
        and anguished aching, morbid spite
    there is no giving to those days
    all functions broken,
    all manners set to die
life moves on in lockstep
we become machines
cranking out our actions blind
        beyond all purpose
        beyond all use
pointlessly running through routines
mindlessly moving through dead modes
            becoming absent within site
            evacuating life in life
            gone to rot before the grave
      some say there is escaping
      in a way
      which takes a death before we die
      but in this lies
      some deeper truth
      some harder pattern than decay
the call rings deep
to turn us off
to find the switch
and take the night
      yet this seems to admit defeat
      or guarantee as by default
      a loss unto the other side
          and we say no
          and we say never
          our stubbornness flares up
          to fight, to grind. and try
somewhere far off we look at this
and pity all that ride through life
      there is no purpose
      there is no good
    when suicide is cast aside
    all our logic is denied
    and we are doomed to further pain
          all this is laughter
          all this is lies
          all this is agony
    when we falter and remain

A NEW-FORGED DARKNESS OF THE SOUL

1
dark streets empty,
hour late,
we take the night
and find it home;
crawling through the underside
of cities far away
still strikes a chord
once cluttered up by fear,
we expand beyond its limits
and encompass all its sides

2
there are no names there,
but stories must abound
beneath the thin veneer
of naked bodies pulsed;
some of these are speaking,
some of these weave tales
of what might be their path to here
and how they come to soak this light
and to ride the doctrines
of the musics of this night

3
the hours move towards changes
and maybe this is change,
somehow a return,
in part reunion with these darks;
but there is difference reigning,
a new forged treaty with the night
beat out in conquering the fear
and stemming weakness
whenever we might find its bane
within our self or in our world

4
we drink up these decisions
but are steeled against the slide,
we know the darkness
and breathe the lateness of its depths,
we ride the silence
and can make of it the sweetest tone;
there is a growing
in this recall,
a stirring purpose
close by the night

ABOUT THESE POEMS

Like my two previous collections, "Into The Dark" and "Amid These Empty Years", the poems in this book represent a selection culled from a particular span of time. However, unlike its predecessors, there were no notably cataclysmic life happenings to break up the flow of my writing, so these 49 poems have a somewhat denser genesis, being pulled from the 500 pieces I wrote in the years 1988 and 1989. Again, I have arranged these in chronological order to present something of the continuity of their composition.

Themes change over time. The writer changes, his access to the Muse changes, and sometimes decays. The accumulation of age and the experience of duration are strange and mostly unexpected things. Existence becomes more set adrift, a constant spot on ever larger canvasses, not really fading but shrinking within context. Contact with the world is less and less an immediate reality and ever more a "Movement Through Depth".

- B.M.T.